THE HORSE LIBRARY

THE HORSE LIBRARY

JUMPING

Betty Bolté

Chelsea House Publishers

Philadelphia

Frontis: **Michael Matz competes in the show jumping competition at the 1996 Olympics in Atlanta.**

CHELSEA HOUSE PUBLISHERS

EDITOR IN CHIEF Sally Cheney
ASSOCIATE EDITOR IN CHIEF Kim Shinners
PRODUCTION MANAGER Pamela Loos
ART DIRECTOR Sara Davis

STAFF FOR *JUMPING*

EDITOR Sally Cheney
ASSOCIATE ART DIRECTOR Takeshi Takahashi
SERIES DESIGNER Keith Trego

CHESTNUT PRODUCTIONS AND CHOPTANK SYNDICATE, INC.

EDITORIAL AND PICTURE RESEARCH Mary Hull and Norman Macht
LAYOUT AND PRODUCTION Lisa Hochstein

http://www.chelseahouse.com

First Printing

1 3 5 7 9 8 6 4 2

Library of Congress Cataloguing-in-Publication Data Applied For.

Horse Library SET: 0-7910-6650-9
Jumping: 0-7910-6657-6

TABLE OF CONTENTS

Two-time gold medal winner, Mark Todd, of New Zealand competes in the 2000 Rolex Kentucky Three-Day Event.

THE ULTIMATE CHALLENGE

Jumping your horse over a challenging obstacle is one of the most exciting and fun aspects of horsemanship, and there are many different equestrian sports that include jumping. Jumping is used during foxhunts, steeplechases, cross-country contests, point-to-point races, trail riding, and show jumping. There's more to jumping, though, than aiming your horse at a fence and hoping you both land safely on the other side. Training for jumping starts with dressage training and endurance conditioning, which are also an important part of one of the most popular equestrian competitions: the Rolex Kentucky Three-Day Event.

A three-day event puts horses and riders through a series of competitions in dressage, in which a horse performs specific movements in an arena; cross country, an outdoor course that requires the horse to jump a series of natural fences and water obstacles; and stadium show jumping. These competitions are combined into one sport known as eventing or three-day eventing. Those who compete in the sport are called eventers or three-day eventers. The different phases of eventing are designed to test the obedience, athleticism, and endurance of the horse, and the horsemanship of the rider. The French term for eventing is Concours Complet d'Equitation, which means "complete equestrian competition" (CCI). The premier three-day events, also known as four-star CCI events, include the Olympics and

The Rolex's Cross-Country Fences

Each year the Rolex course is changed so that it will continue to challenge experienced competitors, as well as encourage new competitors. Course designer Michael Etherington-Smith has developed a worthy course for the Rolex every year since 1992. He also designed the course for the 1996 Atlanta Olympics. Some of the obstacles in the past have included:

NAME	HEIGHT	WIDTH
The Rolex Arch	3' 11"	4'
The Wagon	3' 11"	5' 11"
Porcupines on Lexington Bank	4' 7"	brush
Gazebo Garden	3' 11"	12–15'
Water Trough	3' 11"	5' 6"

the World Championships (each held every four years), the Burghley Horse Trials and Badminton Horse Trials in England, the Adelaide International Horse Trials in Australia, and the Rolex Kentucky Three-Day Event.

The Rolex first became a four-star CCI event in 1998, making it the "youngest" of the four-star, or top-level events. In 2000 the Rolex served as the main competition to select the U.S. Eventing Team that went to Sydney, Australia, for the Olympics.

Now that America has its own four-star competition each year, the country's best riders can compete at the international level at home. This additional experience enhances American chances in other competitions, such as the World Championships and the Olympics.

The Rolex is held at the Kentucky Horse Park in Lexington, Kentucky, on the last weekend in April. This three-day event is actually held over four days, with three days of actual competition for each horse and rider combination. (Each rider may enter more than one horse in the competition.) Each combination must complete the dressage test on their first day of competition, usually a Thursday or Friday. On Saturday, the roads and tracks (phases A and C), steeplechase (phase B), and cross-country (phase D) portions of the event are ridden. These tests show the horse's endurance and speed. Sunday brings the final test: show jumping.

Dressage is not as popular in the United States as it is in other countries, mainly because Americans like to watch fast, exciting sports. You cannot call dressage fast or exciting. However, you can call it elegant, beautiful, graceful, and athletic. As the American public becomes better educated about the basics of dressage, a greater appreciation for the difficulty of the discipline will follow. Even so, the stands at the Rolex are mostly full for the dressage tests on Thursday or Friday.

The focus of the three-day event is the cross-country course on Saturday. Obstacles for the cross-country course include barrels, piles of logs, and even a full-size flatbed farm wagon. The point of this day—through the endurance tests of the roads and tracks, the speedy steeplechase, and the controlled speed of the cross-country course—is to show that the horse is physically capable of the challenges put before him, and that the horse and rider operate as a partnership.

There are many different types of fences and challenges on a cross-country course. The course at the Rolex contains some typical fences, though they are designed to be attractive as well as challenging. For example, one fence is called a ditch and brush. A 5' wide ditch nestles in front of a 4' 7" brush fence, presenting a challenge because the ditch often shakes up the rider more than the horse. Trakehners—a rail suspended over a ditch—are also popular cross-country fences. A hollow, also known as a coffin fence, consists of a rail jump, followed by a ditch and another rail. Step jumps require the horse to jump up or down defined steps on a hill. A chair jump resembles a wide bench with no legs.

These obstacles are designed to test the rider's knowledge as well as the horse's physical abilities. But there is more to a jump than its height and width. The lay of the land surrounding the jump affects how the rider approaches the takeoff. Whether there are trees or bushes around the fence also plays a part in planning how to ride the obstacle. The horses gallop the course at a good pace, so the rider must know what to do before arriving at the fence. Because horses have a mind of their own, a good rider considers alternative strategies should the horse refuse to jump.

Blyth Tait negotiates a challenging water obstacle during the cross-country portion of the Rolex Kentucky Three-Day Event.

Spectators enjoy moving from fence to fence to watch the riders and horses. Cross-country day is a picnicking day, with crowds of people watching the horses, enjoying demonstrations and competitions, and shopping for horse-related goods in the trade show tents.

Some of the world's best eventers compete at the Rolex: Mark Todd, Blyth Tait, Abigail Lufkin, Bruce Davidson,

Karen O'Connor and Regal Scot clear a brush fence during the 2000 Rolex Kentucky steeplechase phase.

Karen O'Connor, and David O'Connor, the 2000 Olympic individual gold medalist in eventing. David O'Connor has even given entertaining dressage demonstrations while riding an inflatable "horse." Competing at the Rolex elevates a rider into the elite of the eventing world.

Mark Todd of New Zealand was named Horseman of the Century in 2000. He has won gold medals at the 1984 Los

Angeles Olympics and the 1988 Seoul Olympics, both times on the same little 15.3 hand Thoroughbred, Charisma. He later wrote a book about their partnership, entitled *Charisma*. He is one of two people to have won the Burghley Horse Trials five times: 1987, 1990, 1991, 1997, and 1999. He has earned the nickname of "Maestro" because of his unique riding style.

Mark Todd joined a pony club when he was nine years old. He enjoyed competing in mounted games, horse trials, and jumping competitions. His first international eventing competition was the 1978 World Championships in Lexington, Kentucky, where he was eliminated on the cross-country course. He has also competed on two Olympic show jumping teams, in 1988 and 1992, finishing among the top twenty competitors. After the 2000 Olympics, Mark Todd retired from eventing, returning to his family farm in New Zealand

You don't necessarily need an expensive horse to com- pete at the Rolex. Joanne Gelarden of Westfield, Indiana, bought a small Tobiano Pinto named Montana Native after a friend saw him in a parade in Wisconsin. She paid only $1500 for him, but he has competed with the best at the Rolex three times and in other high-level competitions, thanks to her dedicated training. Joanne started competing later in life than many eventers, but she has had the courage and determination to succeed in a tough sport. In their first three-day event together in Chicago, they finished in third place. She calls Montana "a very gifted, talented horse." Joanne and Montana were considered for the 2000 Olympic eventing team, but weren't selected to compete.

The other three four-star horse trials are similar to the Rolex, yet maintain their own individual flair. The Mitsu- bishi Motors Badminton Horse Trials are held the first weekend in May in England. The weekend of activities includes the various competitions of the event, as well as a dressage display, horse inspections, band performances, and the presentation of awards at the conclusion of the show jumping competition on Sunday. As with most equestrian events in England, the Badminton is well attended by spectators.

The Burghley Pedigree Horse Trials are held on the first weekend in September each year in England. This event has been held every year since 1961, making it the longest running international three-day event. The Burghley is also one of the most demanding horse trials in the world. One unusual aspect of the dressage test is that it is ridden in a grass arena, rather than a sand arena like the Rolex.

The Mitsubishi Adelaide International Horse Trials occur in Australia on the first weekend in November. The first Adelaide was held at Victoria Park in November, 1997, but that event was the culmination of many years of work.

Event Seat vs. Hunt Seat

There are several positions in which you can ride a horse. In show jumping, the rider assumes a hunter/jumper position. The rider leans farther forward, balanced on his knees, with his weight in his heels. When jumping, his seat is out of the saddle, and his shoulders are forward. The eventer's seat on the flat, however, is deeper in the saddle, with the shoulders slightly behind the hips. The rider's legs wrap around the horse, using more of the calf to hug the horse. When jumping, the eventer's seat is lower to the saddle and more upright, though still leaning somewhat forward.

In 1959 Graham "Kanga" Parham started a horse trials in the town of Gawler, known as the Gawler Three-Day Equestrian Event. In 1986, the World Three Day Event Championships were held in Gawler. In 1997 the Federation Equestre International (FEI), rated the Adelaide a four-star event. The Adelaide combines harness driving trials with their horse trials to broaden the audience. Likewise, they've included local food and wine specialties as part of the cross-country day of festivities. On show jumping day, the Adelaide invites the entire family to enjoy demonstrations of stunt horse riders and Australian stock horses, and to watch the finals of the harness driving trials.

Eventing combines the best elements of several disciplines of equestrian sports that feature jumping. The following chapters take a closer look at each of these sports.

At the advanced level, the cross-country phase of an eventing competition features high and wide obstacles such as log fences and piles.

2

EVENTING
COMPETITION

Modern eventing competition, in which horses and riders
compete in dressage, cross country, and jumping events
that are designed to test their versatility, has its roots in the
training and testing once used to prepare horses for military
use. In Germany, they still call the three-day event the
"Militaire," which was also the name used when eventing was
first included at the 1912 Olympic Games in Stockholm,
Sweden. Horses used by the military needed to be fit enough to
jump natural obstacles across country, cover long distances at
a decent speed, and trust their riders enough to confront any
obstacle presented to them. The sport of eventing grew out of

17

military tests that evaluated a horse and rider's physical fitness, mental ability, and teamwork.

Whether competing at a two-day or three-day event, eventing consists of several phases: dressage; roads and tracks; steeplechase; cross-country; and show jumping. The rider must pace his horse, keeping him fit and ready for another day of challenges. Each phase is included to test the horse and rider in different ways, though the individual tests may seem easier than what you would find at separate competitions. This is because eventing is an all-around competition. For example, the final show jumping compe- tition may seem easier than what you'd see at a Grand Prix, but it follows a difficult endurance test the previous day for the horse. Eventing tests the overall performance and endurance of the horse, not just one aspect of competition.

Two-Day events—as the name suggests—are held over two days and include all phases of eventing. Levels of com- petition include Intermediate and Preliminary. Three-Day events are held over three or more days and have several levels of competition. The levels are indicated by stars (asterisks) after the abbreviation designating the category of the event. A One Star (*) is an introductory competition for riders new to eventing. A Two Star (**) is for riders with a bit of experience in three-day events. A Three Star (***) assumes you have experience competing at the inter- national level, and a Four Star (****) is only for horse and rider teams that have competed successfully at the interna- tional level. The categories tell you how many foreign competitors might be at the competition. A CCN is a National Three-Day Event, a CCI is an International Three-Day Event, and a CCIO is an Official International Three-Day Event. Many FEI rules govern who may compete at these levels, but the phases each draw from the

In steeplechase competition, the goal is to get over the fence quickly, and horses are allowed to brush through the top of the jump.

independent sports of dressage, endurance riding, steeplechase, and show jumping.

The dressage test in an event resembles all other dressage competitions. The horse is being judged on suppleness, obedience, and gaits while it performs specific movements in the arena. The harmony of horse and rider shows in the completion of the required moves: circles, diagonals, turns, etc. Unlike high-level dressage competitions, however, the dressage phase of an event, except in the International Level competitions, doesn't require the horse to perform complicated dressage maneuvers like the piaffe, a calm elevated trot in place, or the passage, a slow motion trot in which the horse moves forward with a degree of suspension in each stride. Depending on the number of entries for the event, dressage rides may occur on one or two days.

The next three phases test the horse's endurance and occur on the second day of the event. Roads and tracks (phase B) resembles endurance riding. The horse trots at a pace of about 220 meters per minute (mpm) ($8^1/5$ miles per

Walking the Cross-Country Course

The day before the cross-country phase of an eventing competition, all competitors are allowed, and strongly encouraged, to walk the course. Pick up a copy of the course map, if one is available, and study it. This is your chance to measure the distance in strides from one fence to the next and to determine your angle of approach to the fence. You can also spot potential problem areas for your horse, whether it's water, or mud, or scary bushes. You are not allowed to take your horse on the course, however. This is where the horse's trust in you becomes evident as he must be willing to jump obstacles he's never seen before. Look out for ground conditions that may injure your horse, such as rocky landings. If you are unsure how to walk a course, have someone more experienced walk with you to help you plan your route and help you memorize the order of the fences.

hour) over a distance of 4,400 to 5,500 meters. This provides a warm-up for the horse, to make sure it is ready for the next phase. Unless your horse pulls up lame during this phase, you go on to the steeplechase.

The steeplechase consists of eight to ten fences. The fences are typically brush, so that the horse can basically jump through the tops of them and clear them quickly. The horse covers the course at a brisk gallop, approximately 690 mpm (25 3/4 mph) over a distance of about 3,000 meters. The steeplechase readies the horse for more jumping to come.

After the horse finishes the steeplechase, he must complete a longer roads and tracks test (phase C). Phase C typically covers 7,700 to 9,900 meters at a comfortable trot. This test helps cool down the horse before it undergoes a mandatory vet check. The horse must be presented to the vet to insure he is sound and able to continue competing. Once the horse has passed the veterinary inspection, he's ready to go to the start box, a large three-sided area where the competitors start the cross-country phase of competition.

Phase D, cross-country, draws many spectators because the horses jump high (and often wide) obstacles. Barrels, log piles, and even flatbed wagons are used as jumps for cross-country. The horse is required to gallop to complete the course within the allotted time, and usually travels about 570 mpm (21 1/4 mph). The number of obstacles, also known as "questions," varies with the course design. Typically, the course consists of about 30 fences. For many horses, the biggest obstacle is the water jump, which has no height, but only width. Water jumps can be imposing, and they tend to stop horses, whether trotting in on the level or jumping down into it. Beginning riders are not usually required to go through water, though it is often given as an option.

The show jumping phase of eventing competition follows the cross-country event and forces the horses to calm down and collect themselves in order to avoid knocking down any rails.

The next day, each rider who completed all previous phases of the event must present his horse(s) for vet inspection again. As long as the horse is sound, the horse may compete in the final phase: show jumping. Show jumping at an event consists of standard jumps with colorful rails arranged within an enclosed arena. It is often difficult for horses to jump a clean round in an arena when they have jumped quickly over large obstacles in a wide-open environment the previous day. Therefore, the show jumping phase tests the horse's willingness to listen to its rider. Many competitors are weeded out during this phase, as one rail down can drop a rider's score significantly.

The U.S. Combined Training Association (USCTA) recognizes six levels of eventing competition: Novice, Training, Preliminary, Intermediate, Advanced, and International Horse Trials. Each level builds on the skills learned in the previous level, so that horse and rider progress toward a perfect harmony, obedience, and suppleness.

Novice is an introductory level for beginning eventers. A subcategory of Novice is Beginner Novice with fewer requirements than Novice. In Novice level competition, the dressage test requires that your horse demonstrate good working gaits (trot and canter) and a good medium walk. You will also perform 10- and 15-meter circles at a trot, encouraging the horse to stretch his neck down on a long rein. The cross-country obstacles are simplistic questions, encouraging the horse and rider to ride fairly aggressively. You only have to jump 12 to 20 jumps, at a comfortable speed of 300 mpm ($11^1/8$ mph). For the show jumping phase, you'll jump 8 to 12 straight or spread fences at about 300 mpm. The maximum height for fences in these phases is 2' 11".

Each level increases in difficulty and complexity. When you reach Training level, you'll need to show that you have more fully developed the walk, trot, and canter, and that your horse can lengthen its stride at the trot and canter. The cross-country course consists of 16 to 22 obstacles with a maximum height of 3' 3". You will be expected to cover the course at about 400 to 450 mpm ($14^7/8$ to $16^3/4$ mph). You may also be faced with a drop, though not deeper than 4' 7".

The jumping phase becomes a little more difficult with the inclusion of two doubles, or a double and triple combination.

Once you reach the Preliminary level, there is a definite increase in difficulty. You must be 14 to compete at this level. You'll now be required to lengthen stride at all three gaits, and perform leg-yielding and shoulder-in. You'll cover the cross-country course at a speed of 520 to 550 mpm (19–20^1/2 mph), jumping 18 to 28 jumps no higher than 3' 7". You'll also encounter spread jumps and drops. The show jumping is at the same height as the cross-country, with 10 to 15 jumps.

Competing at the Intermediate level requires you to be ready for a challenge to your horse, who must be obedient, fast, bold, agile, and able to jump a range of questions. More difficult transitions are required, such as canter-halt and walk-canter. You will also need to be able to turn your horse on his haunches, perform simple changes of lead at a canter, and counter canter (cantering on the off lead). The cross-country phase introduces higher fences—3' 9" high at the maximum. A jump without any height may be 9' 11" wide; with height the fence may be 5' 3" high and 7' 10" wide. You will gallop the course of 12 to 15 questions at 350 to 375 mpm (13 to 14 mph). Drops may be as great as 5' 11". You must be at least 16 years old and an experienced rider to enter this division.

Advanced Intermediate competitions provide a bridge between Intermediate and Advanced competitions. In these types of competitions, the dressage and jumping tests are performed at the Advanced level, while the cross-country test is of the Intermediate level. You must be 16 years old to compete at this level.

The Advanced level is the highest national level of competition. The tests are designed to prepare the horse and

The U.S.A.'s David O'Connor competes on Custom Made during the dressage and cross-country phases of the 2000 Olympic Eventing competition. O'Connor and Custom Made took home the gold medal in individual eventing.

rider for Three and Four Star three-day events of international competition. You must be at least 18 years old to compete. You'll find that the dressage test now demands more from both you and your horse, requiring such advanced moves as the half pass at the trot and canter, and single flying lead changes. The cross-country course asks for greater speed and boldness, and may require you to do bounce jumps into the water. Bounce jumps allow only one stride between fences. The course consists of 25 to 40 questions covered at a speed of 570 to 600 mpm ($21^1/4$ to $22^3/8$ mph). The jumping maximum height is 3' 11" for a solid fence, while spreads can be as great as 9' 2" and a maximum of 5' 11" high. Notice how much higher the fences are at this level. Drops also increase in depth, to 6' 7".

As the level of difficulty increases, so do the risks. Eventers the world over are concerned about the number of deaths associated with cross-country riding. The USCTA is looking into possible causes, ranging from course design, to the required speeds at the higher levels. As competitors and sponsoring organizations look into the issues, they hope to reduce or eliminate deaths while competing.

You must have a good trainer help you learn the proper way to ride, along with good horse management skills, to insure your safety. Having yourself and your horse physically fit and ready to compete is the first priority. You must both be up to the challenges. Your tack must be in good repair and adjusted correctly to be as safe as possible.

One important piece of protective equipment is a safety vest specially designed for equestrians. The safety vest is

Basic Equipment for Eventing

Some tack items are a matter of preference, while others are required. For example, some people prefer a flatter saddle for cross-country. The list of required tack for eventing competitors includes a safety helmet, safety vest, and riding boots. Other essential tack for horse and rider includes a bridle with non-slip reins, a jumping saddle, a saddle pad, a strong girth, a breast collar to hold the saddle in place, galloping boots, bell boots, a crop, and a stop watch.

required for competing on a cross-country course, and is recommended any time that you are jumping. As with any competitive equestrian sport, a helmet is also required.

Other items you'll need for the cross-country phase include galloping boots to protect your horse's legs as he covers the course. Most riders use bell boots over the galloping boots for additional protection. A breast collar helps hold the saddle where it belongs. Special bits, reins, and crops are available.

Remember, have fun riding safely so that you can continue to enjoy riding for many years to come.

Steeplechase jumps consist of gorse fences which the horses are encouraged to jump as quickly as possible.

STEEPLECHASE

The first mention of jumping is found in a French cavalry manual from 1788, making jumping a fairly modern addition to equestrian activities. In 1709, when the laws in England forced landowners to enclose their property, through the Enclosure Acts, property owners planted hedges and built fences and stone walls. The foxhunting crowd could no longer gallop easily across open spaces, and had to jump the hedgerows and walls. As more people realized the exhilaration of jumping during the late 1700s, participation in foxhunts grew. Soon, individuals started comparing how fast their horses could clear the fences between fields. Races emerged, crossing hedges, ditches, and fields. Often these match races between two horses and riders started at one village church and ran to another village church. The steeples of the churches guided the riders from start to finish, thus the name "steeplechase" developed.

The first recorded steeplechase took place in County Cork, Ireland, in 1752, between Cornelius O'Callaghan and Edmund Blake. The two men competed to see whose horse could gallop the four miles from the Buttevant Church to the St. Leger Steeple the fastest. Blake was the winner.

During the early 1800s steeplechasing divided into two styles. The amateur branch became known as point-to-point, while the professional branch remained known as steeplechase. In 1830, the owner of the Turf Hotel in St. Albans founded a steeplechase; 16 horses competed in the first St. Albans Steeplechase.

Steeplechase races are run over fences made of birch, gorse (a spiny yellow-flowered shrub), or hurdles. The Thoroughbreds used in steeplechasing are older animals, often retired from, or not suited to, flat racing. Relatively few stallions and mares compete in this sport.

The world's most famous steeplechase, the Grand National, in Liverpool, England, held its first race on Tuesday, February 26, 1839. The winner was Jem Mason, who rode a 16 hand bay horse named Lottery.

The Grand National, run on the first Saturday in April, consists of 16 fences, 14 of which are jumped twice. Two demanding jumps, the Chair and the Water Jump, are jumped on the first time around the course only. More than 300 horses, 1000 owners, 100 jockeys, and 100,000 visitors attend this three-day affair each year.

The Chair, at 5' 2" high, is the highest fence on the course; it is also the broadest with a ditch that is 6' wide on the takeoff side. Another tough fence is Becher's Brook, named after Captain Martin Becher, who was thrown into the stream at the first race in 1839. The fence is 4' 1" high with a 6' 9" drop on the landing. Though changed in 1989 to make it safer, Becher's Brook is one of the most difficult fences on the course.

Another English steeplechase is the Cheltenham Gold Cup that runs in March during the National Hunt Festival. The fences are made from all natural materials—gorse, birch, and timber. The course consists of 22 fences, varying in height from 2' 6" to 5', and spreads ranging from 6' to 10'. This course is known as the "Olympics" of steeplechase.

Hurdle racing is popular in France. The chief race is the Grande Course de Haies d'Auteuil, with hurdles that reach a height of 3' 6". While the hurdles are lower than in England, a horse can jump through the top of the hedge as he gallops on.

The Grand Steeplechase de Paris, also known as the French Grand National, is held in Auteuil every June. It is

The Wonder of Red Rum

Red Rum was bred to be a sprinter, not a steeplechase horse. As a two-year-old, Red Rum, nicknamed Rummy, was winning races on the flat. In 1972 he was diagnosed with a crippling bone disease, pedalostitis. After an amazing recovery, he went on to win the 1073 Grand National in a record time of 0 minutes 1.0 seconds. He came back to win again in 1974 and 1977, making him the only horse to win the National three times. Red Rum, the most loved horse of the Grand National, died Wednesday, October 18, 1995, and was buried at the winning post on the Grand National course.

Older Thoroughbreds, as well as those that have not performed well at flat racing, are often turned into steeplechase horses.

a four mile course with a wide variety of obstacles. The smallest are a bit bigger than a hurdle, while others are large hedges.

Steeplechasing in the United States hasn't attracted as much attention as in England, but that is changing. The first steeplechase in America took place in 1865. The National Steeplechase Association opened its doors in 1895. Since then, many jump races have been run annually, including the Brookhill Steeplechase, Columbus Steeplechase at Callaway Gardens, Montepelier Hunt Races, Morven Park Steeplechase Races, the Iroquois Steeplechase, and the Virginia and International Gold Cups.

The Virginia Gold Cup is run each year in The Plains, Virginia. This jump race over timber fences has been held annually since 1922. The first race was a four mile flagged course on an estate near Warrenton. In 1924 the race moved to Broadview Estate, in Warrenton, for better viewing by spectators. After the Broadview mansion was destroyed by fire, the race was forced to move again, this time to Clovercroft, with a more difficult course that included more ditches, stream crossings, and steep hills, besides four-foot timber jumps. A few years later, in 1935, the race returned to Broadview. Finally, in 1985 the race moved to its present location. Horses and riders from America and Europe compete in front of 45,000 spectators each year.

Virginia hosts the International Gold Cup on the third Saturday of October. The first International Gold Cup was run in Tennessee in 1903. The course was 4.25 miles long over brush fences. In 1905 the race moved to Rolling Rock, Pennsylvania, and ran there until 1983. Then it moved to Great Meadow Events Center in The Plains, Virginia, where it became a timber race.

Show jumping uses a variety of fences with colorful rails that rest in shallow cups; if the horse touches the rail, it is easily knocked out of the cups and points are deducted.

SHOW JUMPING

S how jumping, like steeplechasing, evolved from foxhunting. In 1865 the Royal Dublin Society's annual horse show in Ireland included, for the first time, competitions in "wide" and "high" leaps. While Grand Prix style show jumping is said to have started in Paris in 1866, at that show the horses and riders paraded on the show grounds, then left and jumped a cross-country style course. The first National Horse Show in the United States was held at Madison Square Garden in New York in 1883.

As evidence of the increasing popularity of jumping, in 1906 Swedish Count Clarence von Rosen suggested equestrian

Riders wear helmets to reduce the chance of serious injury during a fall. Show jumping fences are designed to fall apart upon impact, thereby reducing the risk of injury to both horse and rider. This rider was eliminated from the competition after his horse missed two jumps.

sports be included in the Olympics for the first time. After a couple false starts, equestrian events were included in the 1912 Games. The 1944 Olympics in Paris boasted a total of 99 riders from 17 countries, competing in eventing, dressage, and show jumping. At the 2000 Olympics in Sydney,

Australia, 79 riders from 16 countries competed in show jumping alone.

Most people think of Grand Prix style jumping when asked about show jumping. "Grand Prix" translates from French as "richest or greatest prize" and is used in all sports to mean the most difficult level of competition. Each Grand Prix course is individually designed to present a challenging test.

Of the many horses that attempt a Grand Prix course, only a handful will complete it with a clear (no penalty) round. Those that do finish without any penalties are then eligible to compete in the jump off. The jump off uses some of the same fences as the original course, but is ridden faster and presents an increased challenge.

The first American Grand Prix in show jumping was held in Cleveland, Ohio, in 1965. Through the success of America's show jumping competitors at the 1984 Los Angeles Olympics, 1988 Seoul Olympics, and the 1992 Barcelona Olympics, the sport's popularity has increased dramatically in the United States.

Jumping courses are varied and attractive, often using creative advertising characters as jump standards. For example, Seaworld is a big supporter of show jumping and its fence usually sports two leaping whales holding up the rails. Jumping courses are confined to an arena, and spectators enjoy gathering in their finery to watch and socialize before and during the competition. Prize money is higher in show jumping than in the other disciplines because of the advertising potential. Corporate sponsorships are easily secured, and some Grand Prix competitions are used as charitable fund-raisers.

One popular American show jumping rider is Michael Matz, who has won the United States Equestrian Team

(USET) Show Jumping Championship six times. He competed at the 1976 Montreal and the 1992 Barcelona Olympics, and finally won a team silver medal at the 1996 Atlanta Olympics. Michael Matz has ridden on more than 40 USET squads in Nations' Cup competitions. He won five gold medals at the Pan American Games and took first place in the 1981 Volvo World Cup Final. What he is most known for by the general public, however, is rescuing two young children during a plane crash in Sioux City, Iowa, in 1989; ABC TV named him "Man of the Week" for his bravery. Two weeks later he won the USET Show Jumping Championship. At the 1996 Olympics, Michael was honored to be the first equestrian ever chosen to carry the American flag during the opening ceremonies.

Show jumping courses use brightly colored fence rails to present interesting courses to the horses. Jumps can be 4' 3" to 5' 6" high and are carefully positioned in the arena. The course designer measures the distance between fences to insure the horses can arrive at the fence safely and complete the course within the allowed time. The Grand Prix rider must jump 15 to 20 fences, depending on the course. Faults, or penalty points, are given if a rail is knocked down, if a horse refuses to jump a fence, or if the rider exceeds the optimum time. The rider may be eliminated if he cannot complete the course within the maximum time allowed, or if either the rider or the horse falls (except if competing in a championship). Eliminating a fallen horse or rider is for their benefit—a veterinarian can look over the horse to check for injuries, and the rider can determine if he is hurt and needs assistance.

Smaller show jumping competitions may have between six and fourteen obstacles on a course, and these jumps must be completed within a certain time. As in the Grand

Michael Matz, shown riding Judgement, a Westphalian gelding, has won six USET Show Jumping Championships.

Prix, the winner of any show jumping competition is the horse and rider combination that finishes the fastest with the fewest faults. Some competitions award the win to the combination that finishes fastest and gains the most points during the competition.

Some of the major show jumping competitions include the Nations Cup (held annually), the Pan American Games, the Olympic Games (held every four years), the FEI World

Cup Final (held annually), and the FEI World Championships (held every four years). These competitions are
governed by FEI rules. One rider who recently burst onto
the scene is Rodrigo Pessoa of Brazil. He has won the FEI
World Cup in jumping three times—1998, 1999, and 2000—
each time riding Baloubet du Rouet. Rodrigo Pessoa also
won the FEI World Championships in jumping in 1998 on

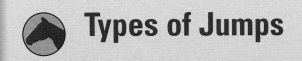 **Types of Jumps**

Vertical: The most difficult type of jump for a horse to gauge
properly. It stands straight up and down, with no spread
width to it.

The Wall: Looks like a solid wall, but the top portions of it
come off easily if hit.

Oxer: separate fences are grouped together to create this
spread jump. The most challenging type is a parallel
oxer.

Triple Bar: Three separate fences are grouped together so
that the first bar is lowest, the second is between the
first and third, and the third bar is highest. While wide,
this type of fence is relatively easy to jump.

Combination: A set of fences with one or two strides
between them.

Water Jump: A long jump averaging 12'-16' with a low
hedge or small fence sometimes defining the takeoff
edge. The landing edge is defined by tape and the
horse must clear it or incur faults.

Gate: A type of vertical jump that looks solid because of
planks, brush, a gate, or rails.

Gandini Lianos. The United States has won the FEI World Championships in jumping team competition only once, in 1986 with Michael Matz on Chef, Conrad Homfeld on Abdullah, Katie Monahan on Amadia, and Katharine Burdsall on the Natural.

Not all championships are for adults. In 1948 the FEI started a Juniors Championship for riders between 14 and 18 years old. Two teams competed that year, one from Italy and one from Belgium. The Italians walked away with the championship.

Horse and rider combinations in America are selected by the USET to compete at international competitions. Therefore, you must be a member of the American Horse Shows Association (AHSA) and of the USET to be eligible for selection. Horses and riders are ranked separately by the USET, based on points earned through competing. Points are awarded by finish (first through twelfth place) and level of competition (local, national, international).

Other types of jumping competition include hunter and jumper classes. The difference between these two jumping classes is easily seen once you know what the judges are looking for. Hunter class judges look for a horse that moves forward easily, without fighting or wringing its tail as it approaches a fence. Hunters are required to jump in a rounded frame—their body must form an arc in the air. The jumps are usually below 4' and appearances count as you jump them. If the rider is in a sloppy position, or if the horse jumps carelessly, twisting its body over the fence, points are deducted from your score.

Jumper classes, on the other hand, are all about speed and clear rounds. Points are deducted only if a rail is knocked down, if a horse refuses a fence, or if the maximum time allowed is exceeded. You and your horse should be neat

Otto Becker and his Holsteiner gelding Cento clear a spread jump at the 2000 Olympics in Sydney, Australia. A spread jump combines two oxers to make a wider jump.

and clean when you enter the show ring, but your horse's jumping style or form is not an issue. Jumper fences are higher, often reaching 5' or more. The Grand Prix is a jumper course.

Horses that are trained for show jumping spend most of their time learning dressage skills. In fact, many of the best jumpers do not practice jumping very much between shows. The rider practices jumping on other horses while the jumper concentrates on dressage, saving his legs for the actual contest.

When schooling your horse, your main objective is to train the horse to respond immediately to your aids. Show jumpers, like all horses, need to know how to carry themselves so that they are light on the forehand (working more from the haunches rather than leaning forward). By using their hind legs to propel them forward, they can turn more easily and are more collected. Jumping is easier as well, as they are engaging their hindquarters more effectively.

Jumpers also need to be able to lengthen and shorten their stride, so you can control how many strides the horse takes before each fence. Too few strides mean a long, flat jump, which will likely knock down the rail. Too many strides mean an emergency half stride right before the fence, which usually causes the horse to pop over the fence like a frog. This can cause the rider to "come out of the tack," or fall off.

Elementary dressage skills that help a horse navigate a jump course include leg yielding, shoulder-in, two-track (half pass), turn on the haunches, and flying change of lead.

Leg yielding teaches your horse to move away from the pressure of a single leg and is the basis for more difficult movements to be taught later. When you apply the aids, your horse will learn to move forward and to the side at the same time. Thus, he will angle from his original track by about a 45-degree angle, with his body still parallel to the original track. This creates four tracks of hoof prints as he crosses his front and hind feet. When you stop applying the aids, he will resume forward movement parallel to the original track.

Shoulder-in is similar to leg yielding, but it makes the horse go forward with his body bent around your inside leg at a slight angle. His hoof prints will form three tracks when this is done correctly.

Two-track is known as half pass in the dressage world. This exercise helps teach your horse to bring his rear hooves farther under his body, lightening his forehand. Despite its name, the hoof prints actually create four separate and parallel tracks.

A dressage move known as the "turn on the haunches" may come in handy when you're competing in a jump off, because it can help you save time by making your turns sharper, while at the same time keeping your horse balanced and under control. By applying specific aids, you ask the horse to swing its forehand in a 180-degree turn around its hindquarters. The hind feet take small steps to stay in one small area while the front feet move. Once your horse knows how to accomplish this, you'll be able to turn him tighter, shaving seconds off your time.

Whether you're competing in a hunter or jumper competition, the course has many turns to approach the fences. Your horse will become unbalanced if he takes a turn at a canter on the wrong (outside) lead. How can you make sure he's on the correct (inside) lead? By asking him to perform

Jumping Stages

The Approach: A good approach is vital to a good jump.

The Take-off: Don't take off before your horse!

Over the Fence: Look straight ahead, not at the jump!

The Landing: As you land, look for the next fence.

The Getaway: Allow your horse to balance himself, then guide him to the next fence.

Michael Whitaker, aboard Prince of Wales, a Hanoverian gelding, attempts a wide triple bar jump at the 2000 Olympic show jumping competition.

a flying change of lead. After you teach your horse to change which leg he leads with, most likely he will perform the maneuver automatically when he's turned in a different direction. Even if he doesn't, though, you can give him the proper cues and he'll be able to keep his impulsion and his balance.

Once your horse knows the basics of dressage, you'll want to school him over fences. When working at home, you want to concentrate on your position and how cleanly your horse jumps. You are building confidence—both in you and your horse. Therefore, only jump 2' or 2' 6" jumps at home. When you're having a lesson with your trainer, she may ask you to jump something higher for experience.

An event horse must be conditioned for maximum suppleness, stamina, and speed. Because thin-skinned, lightly-muscled horses such as Thoroughbreds and Thoroughbred crosses recover faster after a long gallop, they make ideal horses for eventing.

TRAINING AND CONDITIONING

E venting takes nerve. If you feel you have the desire to compete in eventing, you will want to make sure both you and your horse are ready.

If you want to learn how to jump, you must first have a solid seat on your horse. Dressage enables your horse to be strong and supple enough to jump cleanly, so remember to school on the flat before attempting jumping. In fact, you should not try to jump on your own. Especially when you start, have a qualified instructor teach you the proper position for jumping.

If you've been used to competing in hunter or jumper shows, you'll need to relearn your seat. An eventing seat requires that

Although both hunter/jumper and eventer positions require the rider to lean forward, there are noticeable differences between the two seats. The hunter/jumper seat is used for show jumping. The rider leans farther forward, balanced on his knees with his weight in his heels.

your shoulders sit at a slight angle behind your hips, leaning back a bit. This position gives your seat more emphasis on the horse's back and allows you to have better leverage to work with your horse.

Eventers also ride with more lower leg on the horse and less knee grip than hunter/jumper riders. Think of it as hugging the horse with your calves.

The next thing you need to think about is whether your horse is capable of eventing. You'll need a horse that knows how to jump and likes to jump so that you can concentrate on learning what you need to know.

Basic training for an event horse includes training on a lunge line. You (or your trainer) guide your horse through transitions of walk-trot, trot-walk, trot-canter, walk-canter and so on, to help your horse become supple and round. Work your horse in both directions to avoid making him stiff, or one-sided. Your trainer can teach you how to handle the lunge line. It's a good idea to wear gloves when

The event seat is lower to the saddle and more upright, and the rider does not lean as far forward.

you lunge so you don't get rope burns on your hands if your horse pulls suddenly.

You use a lunge line to control your horse's head, and a lunge whip (a very long whip with a long lash on the end) to control the horse's speed. Lowering the whip tells your horse to slow down; raising it a bit tells him to trot; raising it more tells him to canter. You use your voice aid to give verbal commands as you raise and lower the whip. Your tone of voice also gives your horse a clue as to what you want to do. When you say "trot," say it lightly but firmly. When you say "whoa," say it deeper and firmly. Some people use a two-level tone for each command. Thus "trot" becomes "trr-ot" with the second part of the word rising. And "whoa" becomes "who—oa," with the second part of the word falling. Make sure you use the same verbal commands consistently or your horse may become confused.

If you need to find a horse to ride, look for one with a medium-length, slightly arched neck. The horse's shoulders should slope so he can lengthen his stride without too much extra effort. The girth area should be deep, giving the horse plenty of room internally for deep breathing. The

 **Getting Fit**

Remember that your body, not just your horse's, must be fit and conditioned to ride in three-day events. Many eventers work out in a gym or at home. They lift weights to increase their own strength. They do stretches—right before mounting and while mounted—to warm up their own muscles for the ride. Make sure you get enough sleep the night before a competition or a schooling day so you will be less likely to make mistakes.

back should be a medium length for best strength, while a long back tells you that the horse is weaker. The cannon bones should be short. Knees and hocks should be large and the fetlocks should look flat, not round. Check the animal's feet to be sure they are a matched set: rounded in the same way all around. Beware of a horse whose feet turn in or out, or are too small and narrow.

You will need some basic safety equipment, including a safety helmet with attached chin harness, and a pair of flat-soled boots. While it's possible to learn how to jump using an all-purpose saddle, you may find it easier to use a jumping saddle with a forward seat. Adjusting your stirrups a few holes shorter helps shift your weight forward in the saddle a bit, and off your horse's back so he can jump more easily.

You'll need a properly adjusted bridle with as light a bit as you can safely use on your horse. Most horses perform quite well with a simple loose ring snaffle bit. A snaffle is a mild bit consisting of two joined pieces of metal which rest over the tongue. Others need a slightly stronger bit, but too strong a bit in inexperienced hands will harm your horse. Ask a trainer for help in choosing the best bit and bridle for your horse.

Horses can easily injure themselves when cantering to a jump or landing on the other side. Overreach (or bell) boots and galloping (or tendon) boots will protect your horse's front legs as he jumps. If your horse tends to hit his rear legs together as he canters, you might want to put brush boots on his rear legs. Boots also help protect your horse in case he raps his legs into a rail or wall.

Other equipment you might need includes a running or standing martingale, and studs. Martingales are designed to keep your horse's head from rising too high and thus

Because a horse can easily injure itself while jumping or landing, bell boots and tendon boots are worn for protection.

forcing you to lose contact and control. They must be properly adjusted to work correctly, so ask a trainer for assistance. Studs are small attachments for your horse's shoes that give him more traction and help prevent him from slipping.

All tack should fit without hurting your horse; if your horse is in pain, he will not be willing to listen to you.

Your dressage skills will come into play when you ask your pony to arch or round out his back as you approach a jump, making it easier for him to get over the fence without faults. If your horse won't go round for you, he'll need to work harder to clear the fence and often won't make it over. Just as with hunter/jumper training, eventing horses must learn dressage to keep them listening and responsive. Of course, eventing horses are also required to perform a dressage test, so they must know the elementary dressage skills. Eventing isn't just about speed and daring, it's about the partnership between horse and rider, which dressage develops. An event horse is conditioned with a combination of techniques used by endurance riders, jumping riders, and fox hunters.

If you want to condition your horse for show you must pay attention to his nutrition. Your horse must receive a proper diet to perform well. Sufficient good quality hay is a must. As your horse works harder, you'll probably need to give him some grain as well. How much grain depends on how "hot," or energetic, your horse is. You'll need to ask your trainer or someone knowledgeable about feeding horses for advice on your horse's dietary needs.

You also need to provide turn-out, time spent in the pasture, for your horse, so he doesn't spend all day in a stall. Being in a pasture helps calm a horse, and it exposes him to different sounds and sights.

To help your horse grow stronger, with more endurance, you will have to slowly increase the amount of stress included in his workout. You can increase your horse's lung capacity and heart capacity in six months of proper conditioning; his tendons and ligaments in one to two years; and his bones in three years. But you must do this gradually so that you do not strain or injure your horse. Endurance riders use a technique called LSD: long, slow, distance work. Eventers typically use interval training to condition horses. That is, alternating between two or three types of exercise within one workout, just as human athletes do.

Use a stethoscope to become familiar with your horse's resting heart rate. Normally, this rate falls between 32–40 beats per minute (BPM). If your horse's rate is lower than this, he has a strong heart muscle already and should be wonderful at cross-country. To determine your horse's normal respiratory rate, watch his flank rise and fall near the stifle (in front of his hip) and count each rise for 15 seconds. Multiply by 4 to obtain the respiratory rate. A resting rate is typically 2–20 breaths per minute. One last vital sign you should know for your horse is his temperature. To take a horse's temperature, put a little petroleum jelly on the end of a rectal or veterinary thermometer, and insert it into your horse's rectum. Tying a string to one end of your thermometer and attaching a clip to the other end of the string is recommended. Putting the clip on the horse's tail eliminates any danger of losing the thermometer inside the horse should he startle. The normal temperature for an average horse is 99–101 degrees Fahrenheit.

To determine your horse's current level of conditioning, ride your horse for an hour in a good workout. Dismount and immediately check his heart rate. Check it again in a few minutes and continue to do so until the heart rate is down to 64 BPM. If it takes 30 minutes or more for him to reach this heart rate, you are working him too hard. However, if he recovered in 10 minutes or less, you are not working him hard enough. Monitoring his heart rate recovery period is one way of ensuring you're gradually increasing the conditioning program to build up your horse's strength and endurance.

Your conditioning program should have three parts: cardiovascular, strength, and suppling. The cardiovascular training helps the heart and circulatory system, the respiratory system, and the muscular system to efficiently produce energy, increasing your horse's stamina. Strength training raises the level of endurance and the power of the horse's muscles. Suppling helps your horse move more easily and become more athletic, thus reducing the risk of injury.

While your horse's strength and suppling improve naturally as you train him through dressage, cardiovascular training requires some special work. This is where LSD (long, slow, distance work) comes into play. By walking, trotting, and cantering slowly for increasingly longer periods

What to Watch Out for When Jumping

The most common problems for beginning jumpers include:

- losing contact with the horse's mouth right before takeoff
- leaning too far forward or to the side
- taking off before the horse or being left behind
- looking at the ground instead of the next fence
- swinging the lower leg
- resting on the horse's neck
- thumping back into the saddle on landing

A trainer can help you to correct these errors so that jumping is as safe as possible for both you and your horse.

of time, you will improve your horse's condition. Normally, the LSD program begins with 20 minutes of walking. Gradually introduce trotting and cantering until you're cantering a total of 20 minutes, though not all at one time. Then over the next 6–8 weeks, you'll increase the total workout time to $1^1/2$–2 hours.

Eventers use interval training, which is best for high-performance horses. For example, you might walk for 10 minutes, then trot for five, then canter for two, to begin with. Over the following weeks, each segment is lengthened and then repeated until your workout is the length you need. By walking between short periods of trotting, cantering, and galloping, you allow your horse's system to recover and rest a bit.

A typical program includes one day of hard workout, where the horse is cantered and sometimes galloped, every third or fourth day. Between hard days, include dressage and jumping sessions, increasing the difficulty to the hard workout day.

If you have gentle hills where you can ride, you'll want to use them to help strengthen your horse's ligaments. Whenever possible, take your horse to new surroundings. Not only does this help him adjust to being in different places, it also keeps his interest and prevents him from becoming bored.

In eventing you will encounter show jumping and cross-country jumping, each with its own kinds of fences and approaches. Show jumping takes place in an arena, and the jumps vary in size and type. However, the show jumping portion of an eventing competition will be much less difficult than a traditional show jumping competition.

Cross-country fences vary greatly in size and appearance. Schooling is more difficult because there are fewer places that have cross-country fences. You can build some cross-country jumps yourself. Try to vary their appearance from time to time to present a new question (obstacle) to your pony.

One type of cross-country fence that you can create using show jumping equipment is a coffin jump, a three-part jump in which the first fence is two strides from a ditch, which is one stride from another fence. You can also stack up a few straw bales between two jump standards and place a ground pole in front of the stack, and a pole above the bales. Barrels are easily found at industrial and automotive centers. Once you clean and paint them, you can lay them on their sides (anchored in place) and lay poles across them, or form a cross-pole (an X-shaped) jump over them. You can also try making an arrowhead, or corner, jump. You jump across this V-shaped jump, not into it. Most riders aim for the center or the narrowest part of the V to jump. To make the jump, place three barrels or upside-down buckets on their sides, forming a 45-degree triangle. Lay three poles on top of the barrels, connecting them. Make sure you put ground poles at the base of each leg of the corner so the horse has a ground line to use to judge its takeoff.

Trail riding is also good schooling for cross-country. You may come across a fallen log that has a clear approach and landing, or a small stream that can be splashed through or jumped.

For many horses the greatest challenge is a water jump. Some are not afraid of it, others fear monsters lurk within the depths. Resisting walking through water is natural to a horse, so don't get upset with your horse if she refuses. Encourage and calm your horse, and most of all be patient as you present the water obstacle to your horse. With time and patience, your horse will come to accept the obstacle, realize that it won't hurt her, and easily walk through.

One of the best sets of equipment for training your horse for jumping are cavaletti. Cavaletti are poles that are placed on the ground or slightly raised, at specified intervals about one trotting stride apart. Riding in two-point (jump) position, you trot over one to seven poles, forcing the horse to pick up its feet with coordination to avoid hitting the poles. This builds up the horse's muscles. Slightly raised cavaletti force the horse to pick up its feet higher. Your trainer can help you to develop appropriate exercises for you to work on between lessons.

Another technique is grid work. A grid is a set of jumps placed in a row, usually one or two canter strides apart. They are usually all the same height. The idea is to ride straight through the jumps, keeping your pony in the middle of each jump. Your trainer or a friend can watch from the side, see your jumping position clearly, and observe how the horse or pony is jumping. This enables her to correct your position and correct any problems your mount may be having. Grids can also train a horse to jump combination jumps.

Measuring Your Pony's Pulse

Put a stethoscope along the horse's left side, at the girth area, just behind and above the elbow. Listen for a "lub-dub" sound, one heart beat. Count these beats for 15 seconds. Multiply by 4. That's the number of beats per minute.

One aspect of training and conditioning for eventing that no one can teach you is heart. You must have the courage to trust your horse to carry you over each obstacle. An old saying about jumping is that if you "throw your heart over the fence, the horse will follow." Imagine yourself and your horse clearing each fence cleanly, and most likely you will. Enjoy your ride!

1752	The first steeplechase match is held in County Cork, Ireland
1788	The first mention of jumping appears in a French cavalry manual
1839	The first Grand National Steeplechase is held at Aintree in Liverpool, England
1865	Jumping is added to the Royal Dublin Society's annual horse show in Ireland
1910	The first international show jumping competition is held in Buenos Aires, Argentina
1912	Three-day eventing is included in the Olympic Games at Stockholm, Sweden
1923	The British Show Jumping Association is founded
1978	World Three-Day Event Championships are held at Lexington, Kentucky, leading to the creation of the Rolex Kentucky Three-Day Event (CCI***)
1978	The FEI recognizes endurance riding as a sport
1986	The World Three-Day Event Championships are held in Gawler, Australia
1997	The Gawler Three-Day Event becomes a CCI**** known as the Mitsubishi Adelaide International Horse Trials
1998	The Rolex Kentucky Three-Day Event becomes a CCI****, the only four-star competition in the Western Hemisphere
2000	USET member David O'Conner wins the individual gold medal in eventing at the Sydney Olympics; the U.S. team takes the bronze medal in eventing

GLOSSARY

Aids—cues that tell a horse what to do; natural aids include voice, hands, legs, and seat; artificial aids include whips and spurs

Bounce jump—an obstacle with a fence one stride away from another

Cavaletti—poles that are placed on the ground or slightly raised and used to build up a horse's muscles for jumping

Clear round—term used to describe a a show jumping course completed without knocking down any rails from the jumps, refusing or running out at a fence, or exceeding the course time allotment

Double—two obstacles jumped in succession

Drop—when the horse is required to jump down from a flat surface

Fault—penalty points given to a horse and rider when they make a mistake, usually four or five points for each fault.

Gorse—a spiny yellow-flowered shrub used as brush in a steeplechase fence

Ground poles—poles placed on the ground in a row over which the horse can trot or canter; are also used to help a horse learn to pace itself when approaching a jump

Lunge line—a long, usually flat lead line that attaches to the horse's bridle that is used to train a horse on a 20-meter circle, with or without a rider

One-sided—term used to describe the condition of a horse that can bend easily to one side only

Questions—any obstacle on a jumping or cross-country course

Rump rug—a short blanket that is laid over the horse's haunches to keep the muscles warm

Scapula—shoulder blade

Stiff—term used to describe the condition of a horse that has a hard time bending on one side

Triple—three obstacles jumped in succession

Benson, Gary and Phil Maggitti. *In the Irons: Show Jumping, Dressage, and Eventing in America.* New York: Howell Book House, 1994.

Binder, Sibylle Luise & Gefion Wolf. *Riding for Beginners.* New York: Sterling Publishing Co., Inc., 1998.

Budd, Jackie. *The Complete Guides to Horses and Ponies: Horse & Pony Jumping.* Milwaukee, Wisconsin: Gareth Stevens Publishing, 1999.

Draper, Judith. *Practical Showjumping.* New York: Ward Lock, 1993

Holderness-Roddam, Jane. *Fitness for Horse and Rider.* Devon, UK: David & Charles Publishers, 1993.

Loriston-Clarke, Jennie. *Illustrated Guide to Dressage.* New York: Viking Penguin, 1988.

Smart, John. *Showjumping: Preparation, Training and Competition.* New York: Howell Book House, 1987.

Stoneridge, M.A., ed. *Practical Horseman's Book of Riding, Training and Showing Hunters and Jumpers.* New York: Doubleday, 1989.

Strickland, Charlene. *Show Grooming: The Look of a Winner.* Ossining, New York: Breakthrough Publications, 1995.

Websites

www.ahsa.org
American Horse Shows Association

www.uset.com
United States Equestrian Team

www.horsesport.org
Federation Equestre Internationale

www.rk3de.org
Rolex Kentucky Three-Day Event

www.aintree.co.uk/website
Martell Grand National

BETTY BOLTÉ lives on a mini horse farm in Canton, Georgia, with her husband, her two children, and her father. Her daughter Danielle is training to compete in eventing. Mrs. Bolté has loved horses since she was a little girl and has attended horse shows throughout her life for the simple joy of watching horses perform. A graduate of Indiana University, Mrs. Bolté is the also the author of *Hometown Heroines*, a collection of historical biographies of 19th century American girls.